Facts About the Koala

By Lisa Strattin

© 2019 Lisa Strattin

FREE BOOK

FREE FOR ALL SUBSCRIBERS

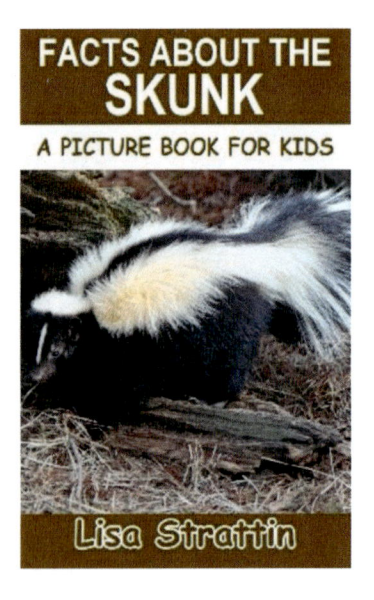

FACTS ABOUT THE SKUNK

A PICTURE BOOK FOR KIDS

Lisa Strattin

LisaStrattin.com/Subscribe-Here

BOX SET

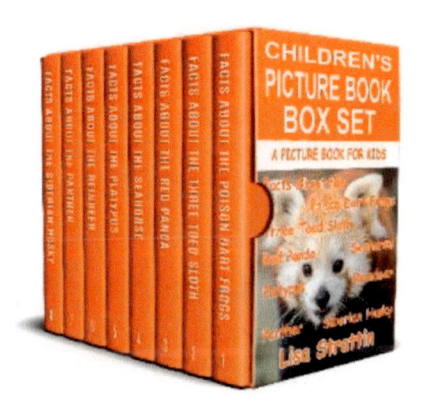

- **FACTS ABOUT THE POISON DART FROGS**
- **FACTS ABOUT THE THREE TOED SLOTH**
  - **FACTS ABOUT THE RED PANDA**
  - **FACTS ABOUT THE SEAHORSE**
  - **FACTS ABOUT THE PLATYPUS**
  - **FACTS ABOUT THE REINDEER**
  - **FACTS ABOUT THE PANTHER**
- **FACTS ABOUT THE SIBERIAN HUSKY**

LisaStrattin.com/BookBundle

Facts for Kids Picture Books by Lisa Strattin

Little Blue Penguin, Vol 92

Chipmunk, Vol 5

Frilled Lizard, Vol 39

Blue and Gold Macaw, Vol 13

Poison Dart Frogs, Vol 50

Blue Tarantula, Vol 115

African Elephants, Vol 8

Amur Leopard, Vol 89

Sabre Tooth Tiger, Vol 167

Baboon, Vol 174

Sign Up for New Release Emails Here

LisaStrattin.com/subscribe-here

All rights reserved. No part of this book may be reproduced by any means whatsoever without the written permission from the author, except brief portions quoted for purpose of review.

All information in this book has been carefully researched and checked for factual accuracy. However, the author and publisher makes no warranty, express or implied, that the information contained herein is appropriate for every individual, situation or purpose and assume no responsibility for errors or omissions. The reader assumes the risk and full responsibility for all actions, and the author will not be held responsible for any loss or damage, whether consequential, incidental, special or otherwise, that may result from the information presented in this book.

All images are free for use or purchased from stock photo sites or royalty free for commercial use.

Some coloring pages might be of the general species due to lack of available images.

I have relied on my own observations as well as many different sources for this book and I have done my best to check facts and give credit where it is due. In the event that any material is used without proper permission, please contact me so that the oversight can be corrected.

COVER IMAGE

https://flickr.com/photos/145874413@N08/32259440831/

ADDITIONAL IMAGES

https://flickr.com/photos/albert_straub/22053247510/

https://flickr.com/photos/hkxforce/2174831889/

https://flickr.com/photos/bigblueocean/2756184910/

https://flickr.com/photos/frank-wouters/10108174/

https://flickr.com/photos/26934954@N02/4479221075/

https://flickr.com/photos/bigblueocean/2756160520/

https://flickr.com/photos/janusserendipity/6937350840/

https://flickr.com/photos/davidstanleytravel/32249661518/

https://flickr.com/photos/sdstrowes/3917299626/

https://flickr.com/photos/labutacadorada/17501246054/

Contents

INTRODUCTION 9

BEHAVIOR 11

APPEARANCE 13

LIFE CYCLE 15

LIFE SPAN 17

SIZE 19

HABITAT 21

DIET 23

ENEMIES 25

SUITABILITY AS PETS 27

INTRODUCTION

The Koala is a small- to medium-sized mammal that lives in different types of forests in southeastern Australia. Despite its appearance and the fact that it is also known as the Koala Bear, Koalas are really marsupials. Although they are considered one of Australia's most memorable animals, when European settlers first arrived, things were very different. There were millions of Koalas killed every year for their fur.

Today, as of this writing in 2019, although populations are stable, the Koala is affected by habitat loss as vast areas of land are cleared every year to support growing development.

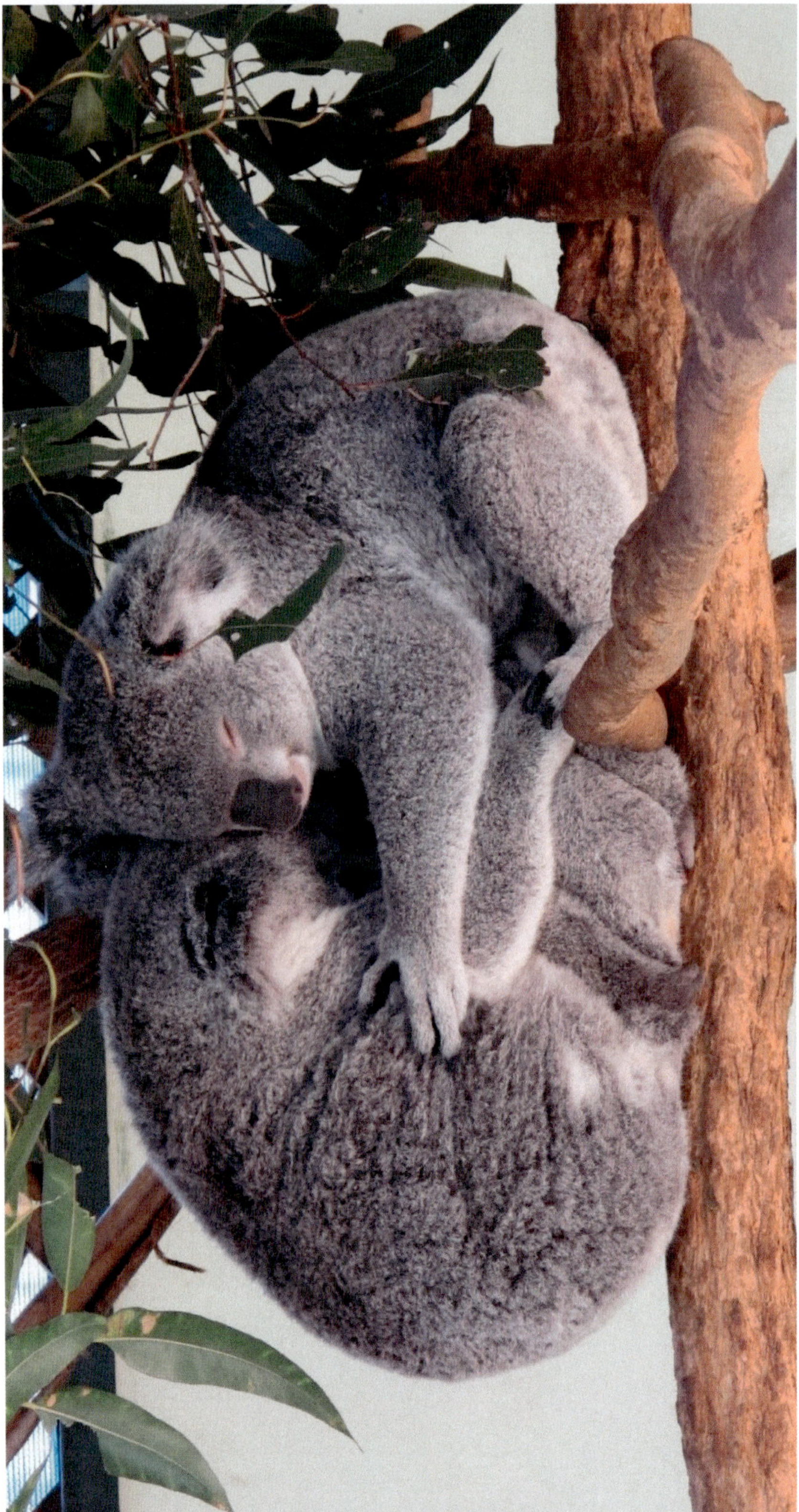

BEHAVIOR

The Koala is solitary and nocturnal spending most of the daytime hours sleeping in the fork of the eucalyptus tree. Their low-energy leads to them leading an inactive lifestyle because they are happy to spend up to 18 hours a day sleeping or just sitting in the trees. Everything from sleeping to eating and even breeding is done in the trees and when they do come down, it is only to move to another tree.

Koalas are also sedentary animals which means that they live in a fixed home range which only varies based on the amount of available food. Though the home ranges of males and females overlap, males will not tolerate rival males coming into their territory and will fight intruders viciously by scratching and biting them.

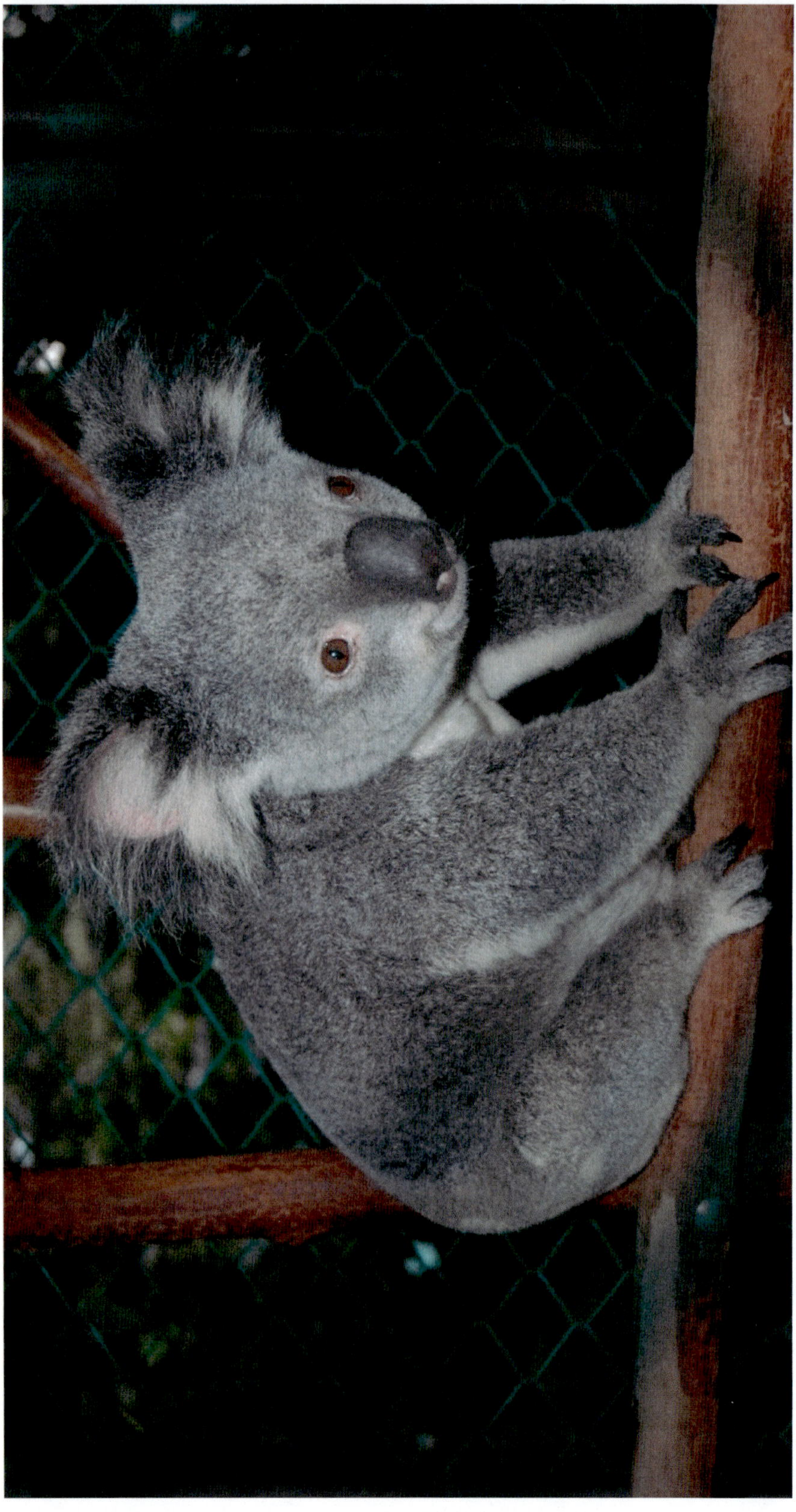

APPEARANCE

The Koala is one of the most charismatic of all marsupials with its large, wide face and round, white-tufted ears. They don't have a visible tail, but a smooth, black nose which also adds to it having the appearance of a small bear. They have dense, soft grey or grey-brown fur which is lighter on their underside and mottled on the rear. They have short, powerful limbs that are tipped with sharp claws. The two opposable thumbs and three fingers on each hand help them to grip onto even the smoothest bark when climbing and eating in the trees. They move around in the trees by jumping, then moving both their back legs up the tree together, allowing them to get higher.

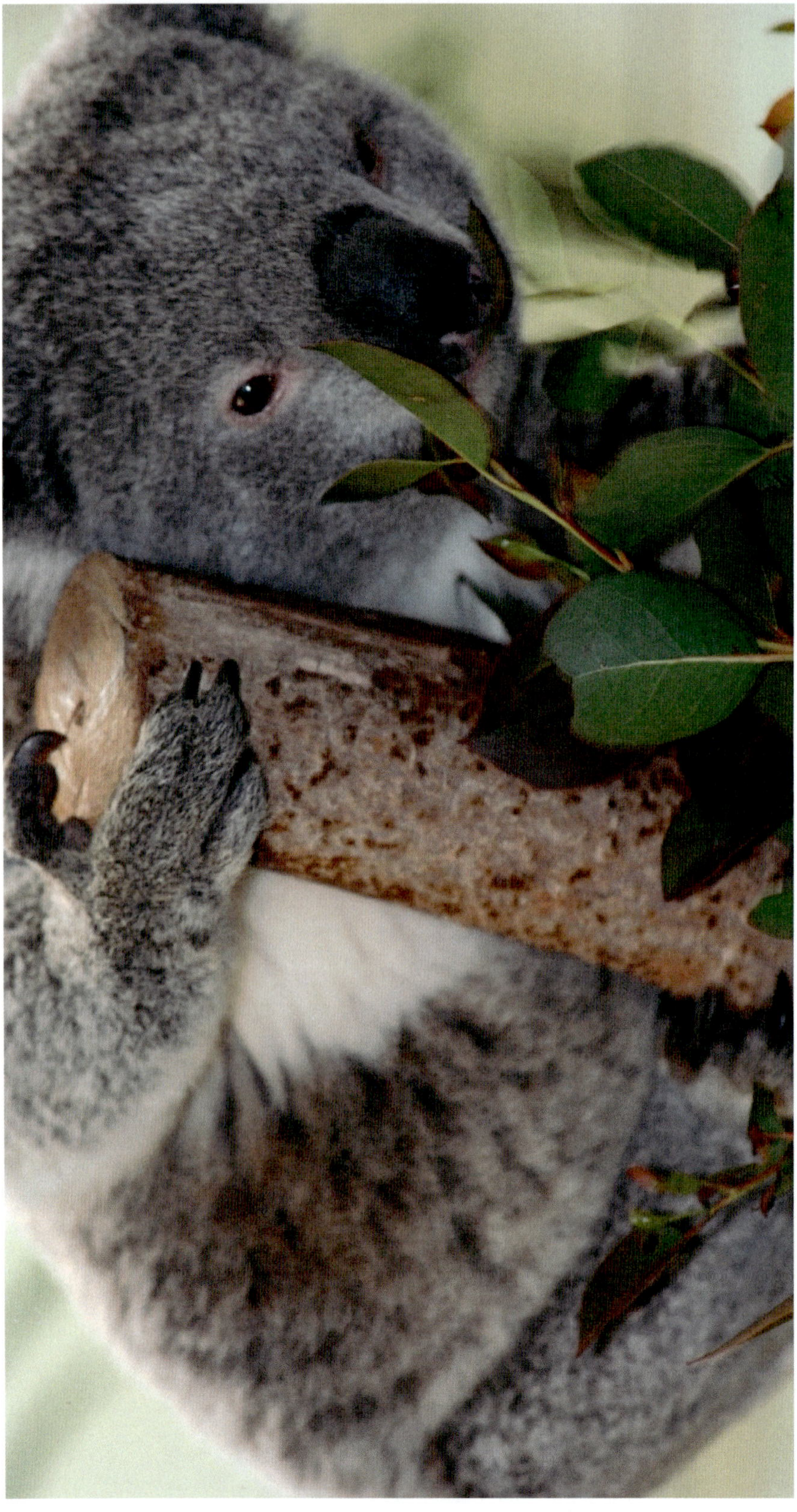

LIFE CYCLE

During the breeding season, males can be heard making loud calls through the forest to both attract a female and also to warn off any rivals. In their society, the dominant male gets to mate with the most females. They are able to reproduce from the age of two years old, but breeding is not usually successful until the male is between 4 and 5 years old and has established dominance in his home range.

The female is pregnant for only 35 days, then a single joey is born that is about the size of a bee. The baby is very underdeveloped, and immediately crawls into the pouch on the mother's belly. The joey stays in the pouch until it is weaned at between 6 and 7 months old. The young Koala then holds onto the mother's back where it stays for another few months. Sometimes it is forced to leave because another joey is ready to leave the pouch and take the place on the mother's back.

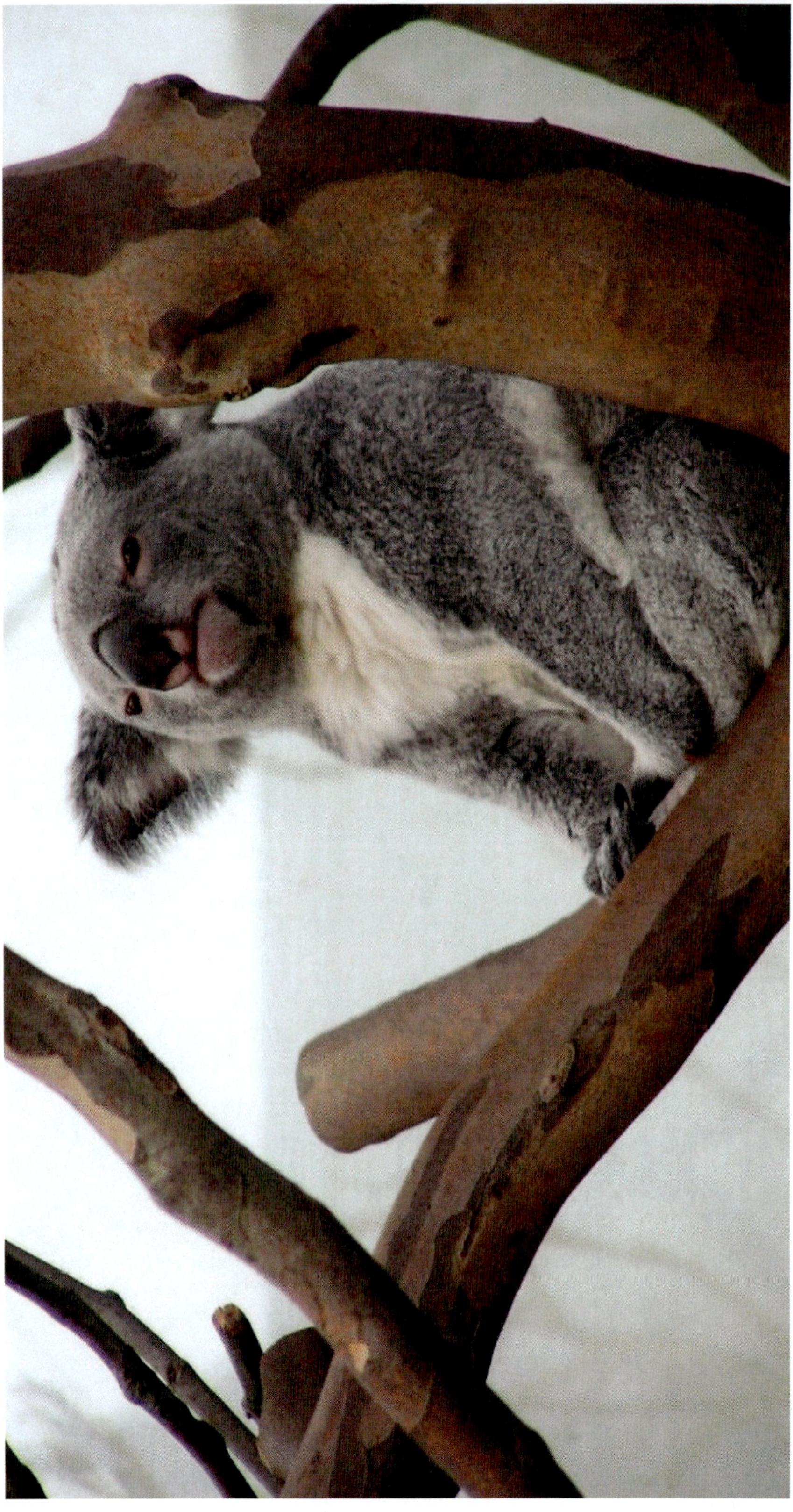

LIFE SPAN

Koalas live for 15-20 years on average.

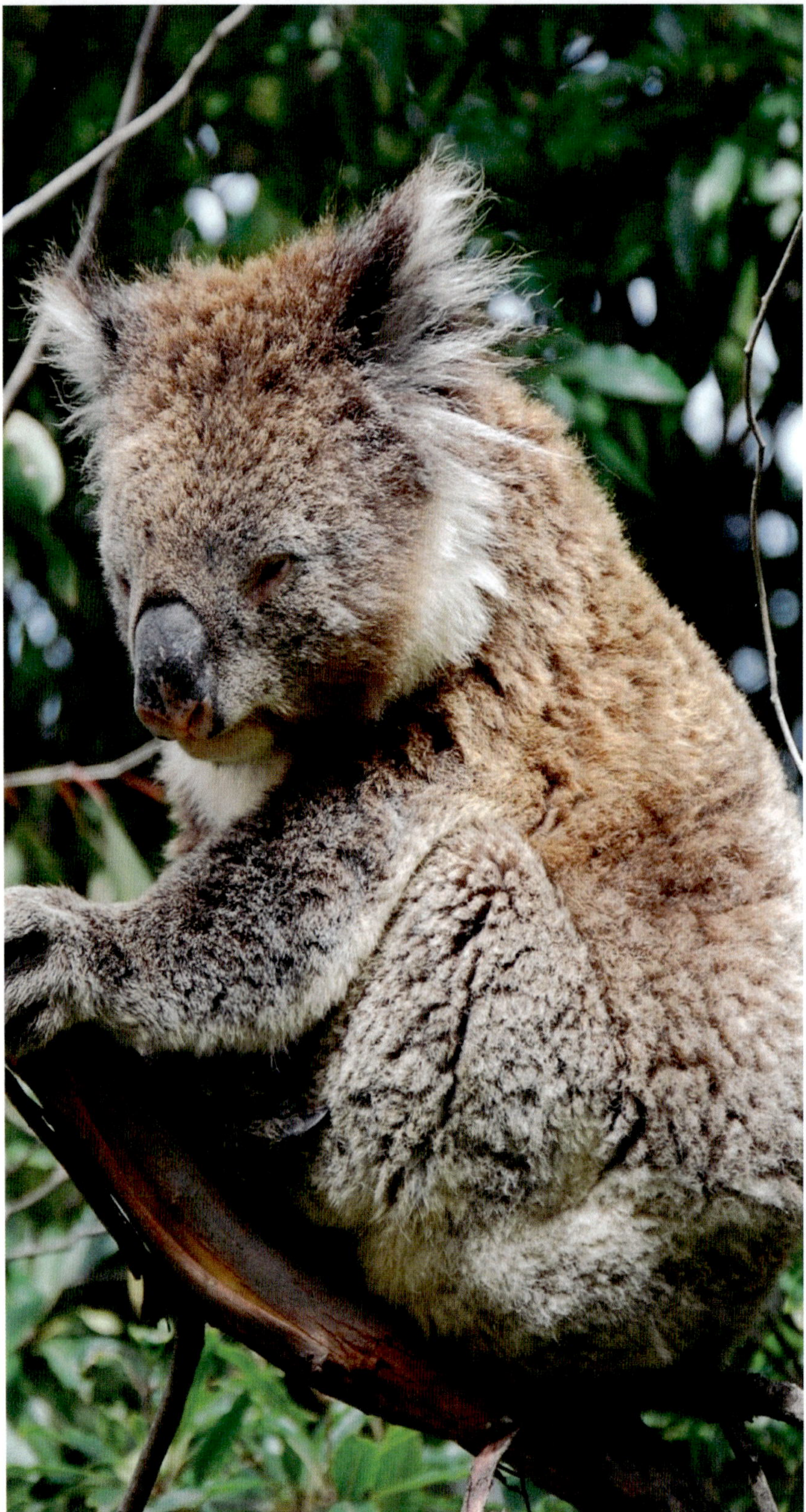

SIZE

Koalas grow to be 2 to 3 feet tall on average and weigh from 8 to 33 pounds.

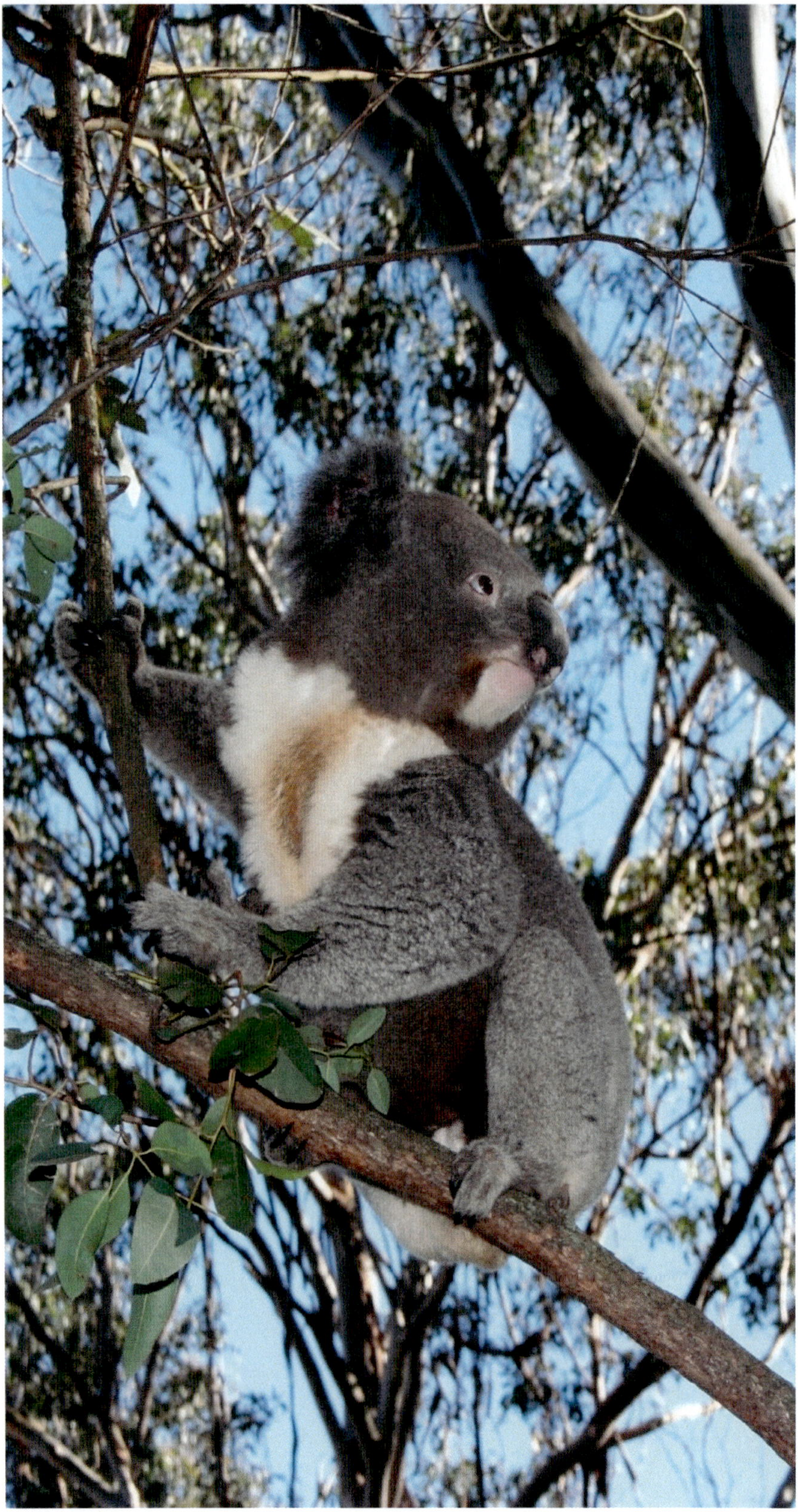

HABITAT

Even though many Koalas were killed by hunting, they are quite resilient and live in many different forest environments, from the tall eucalyptus forests to coastal regions and even low-lying woodlands further inland. They have large populations in much of their natural range today, but fires and land clearance by people has meant a loss of their habitats and separates them, keeping them isolated from other groups.

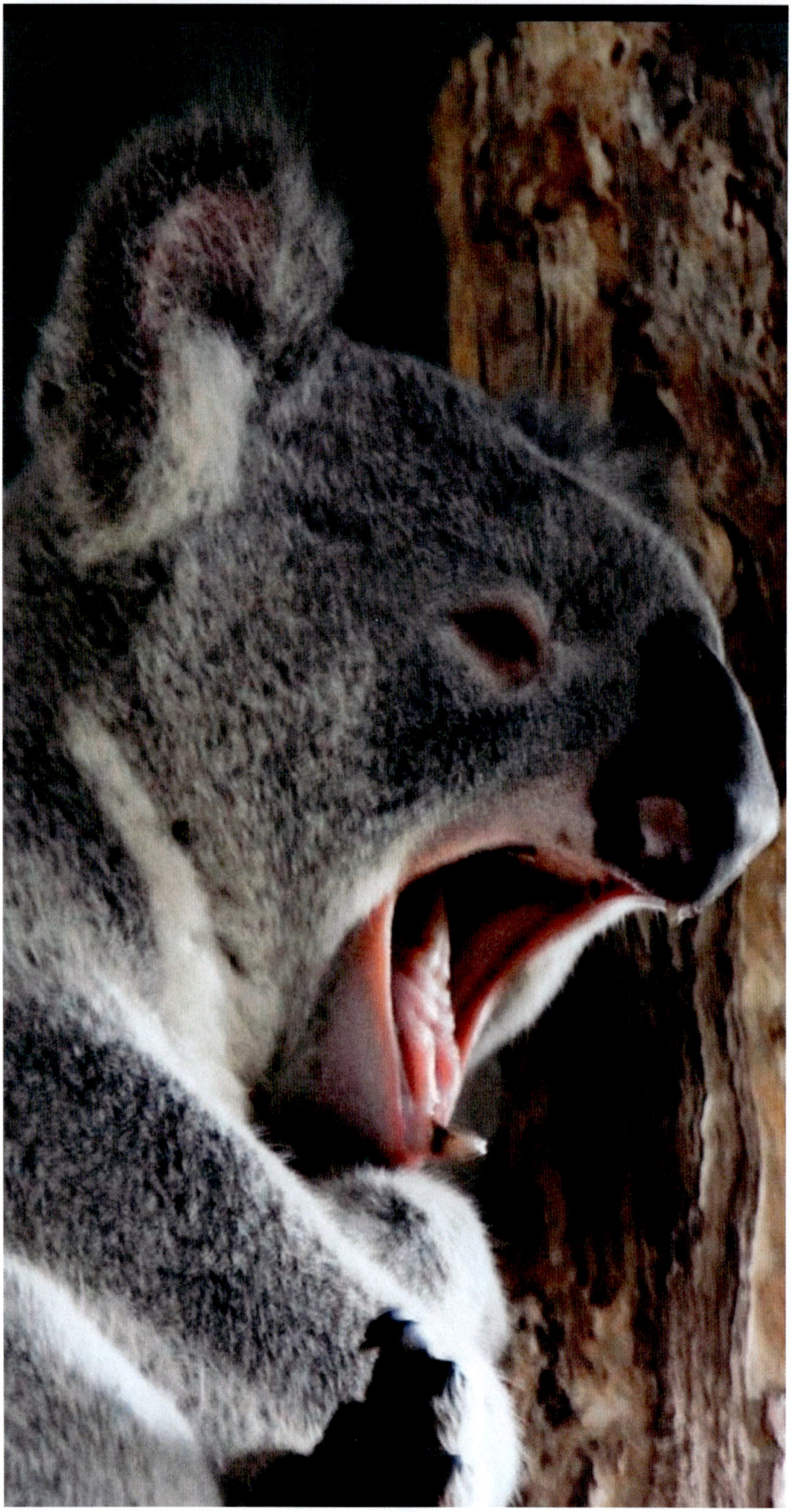

DIET

The Koala is a herbivore that only eats the leaves of the eucalyptus (gum) tree. There are around 600 different species of eucalyptus, but Koalas only seem to feed on 30 of them, depending on what is in their home habitat. Eucalyptus leaves are tough, fibrous and often toxic. This makes them inedible to many other animals. The Koala has evolved to be the animal that eats them, they have large cheek pouches where the leaves are stored. Once the cheek pouches are full, the Koala begins to grind the leaves down into a pulp using flat cheek teeth, causing some of the toxins to be being detoxified by their liver, making the leaves safe for them to eat.

The Koala also has digestive tract (the way the food travels through their body) more than three times its body length to help break down the tough leaves. Koalas are also known to eat soil, bark and gravel to aid in the digestion of the fibrous plant.

They get almost all of the water that they need through their food.

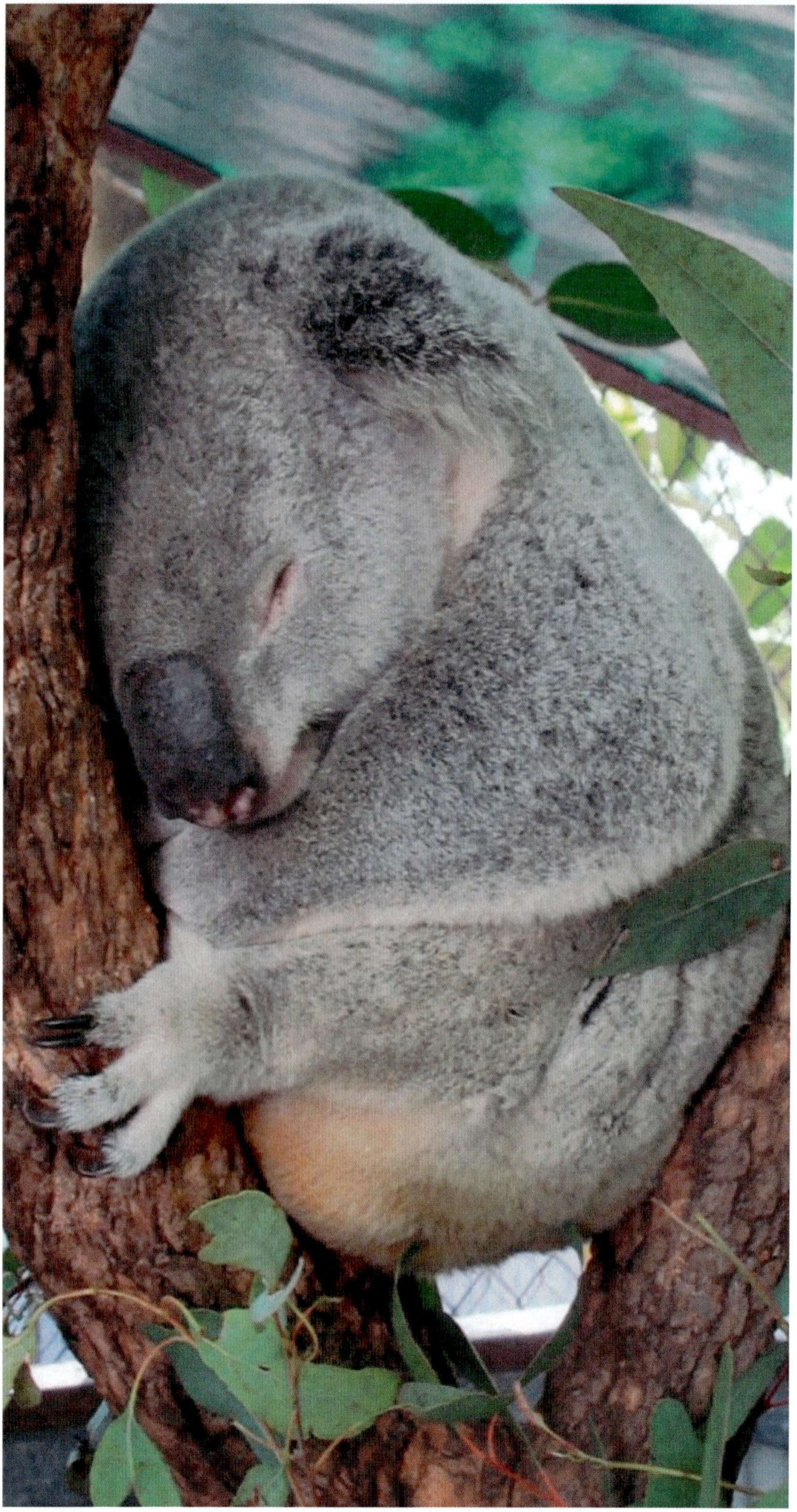

ENEMIES

Despite being relatively small, the adult Koalas have very few natural predators with the exception of large Birds of Prey. Young Koalas are vulnerable to be preyed upon by more animals, including snakes., Adults and young are most threatened by domestic animals, particularly dogs, that not only attack them but also spread disease into local populations.

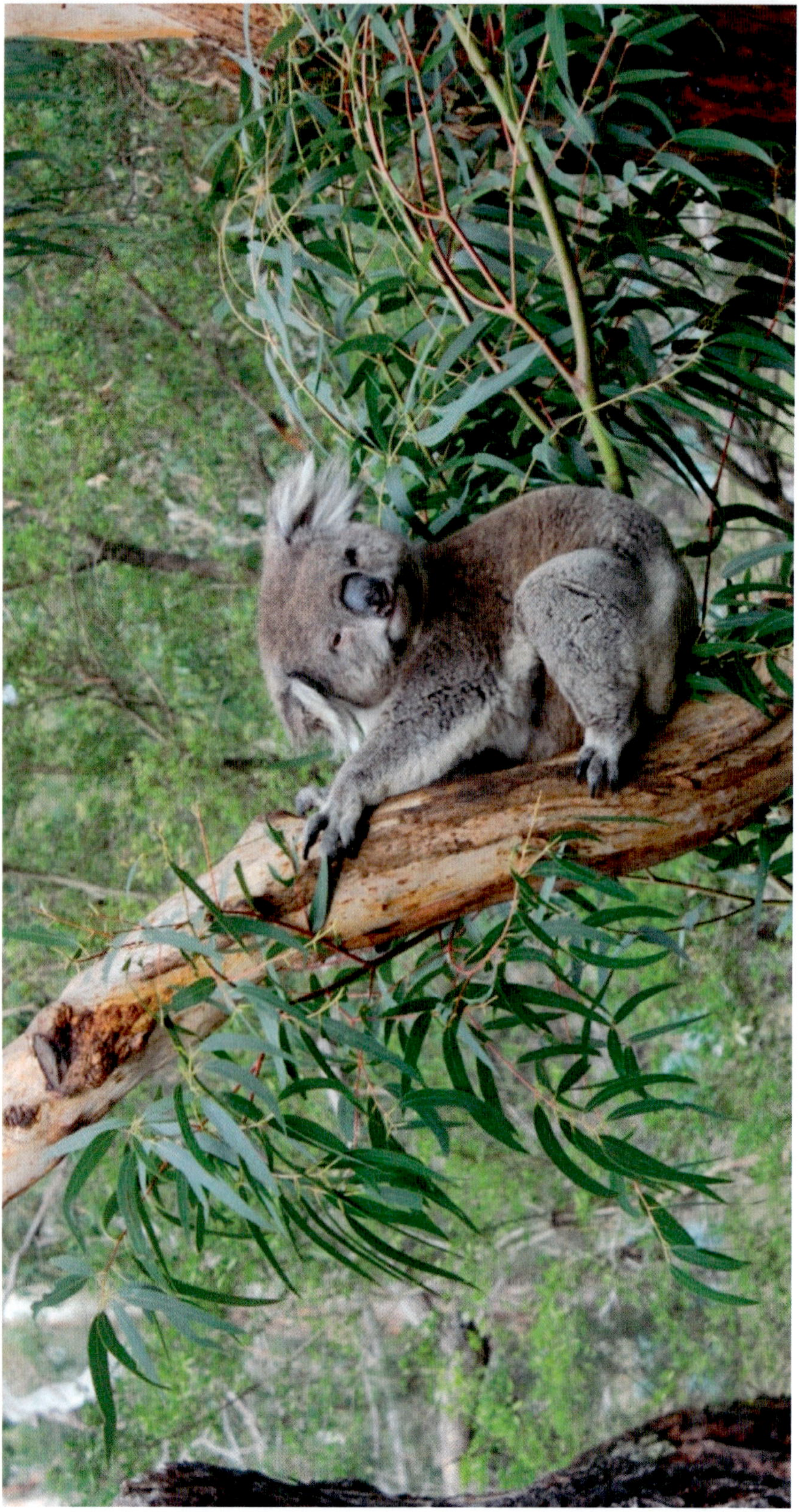

SUITABILITY AS PETS

The Australian Koala Foundation says it's illegal to keep a koala as a pet anywhere in the world! Not even Australians can own one.

But there are some exceptions. Authorized zoos can keep koalas, and occasionally scientists can keep them in order to study them.

You can visit a zoo and see some Koalas.

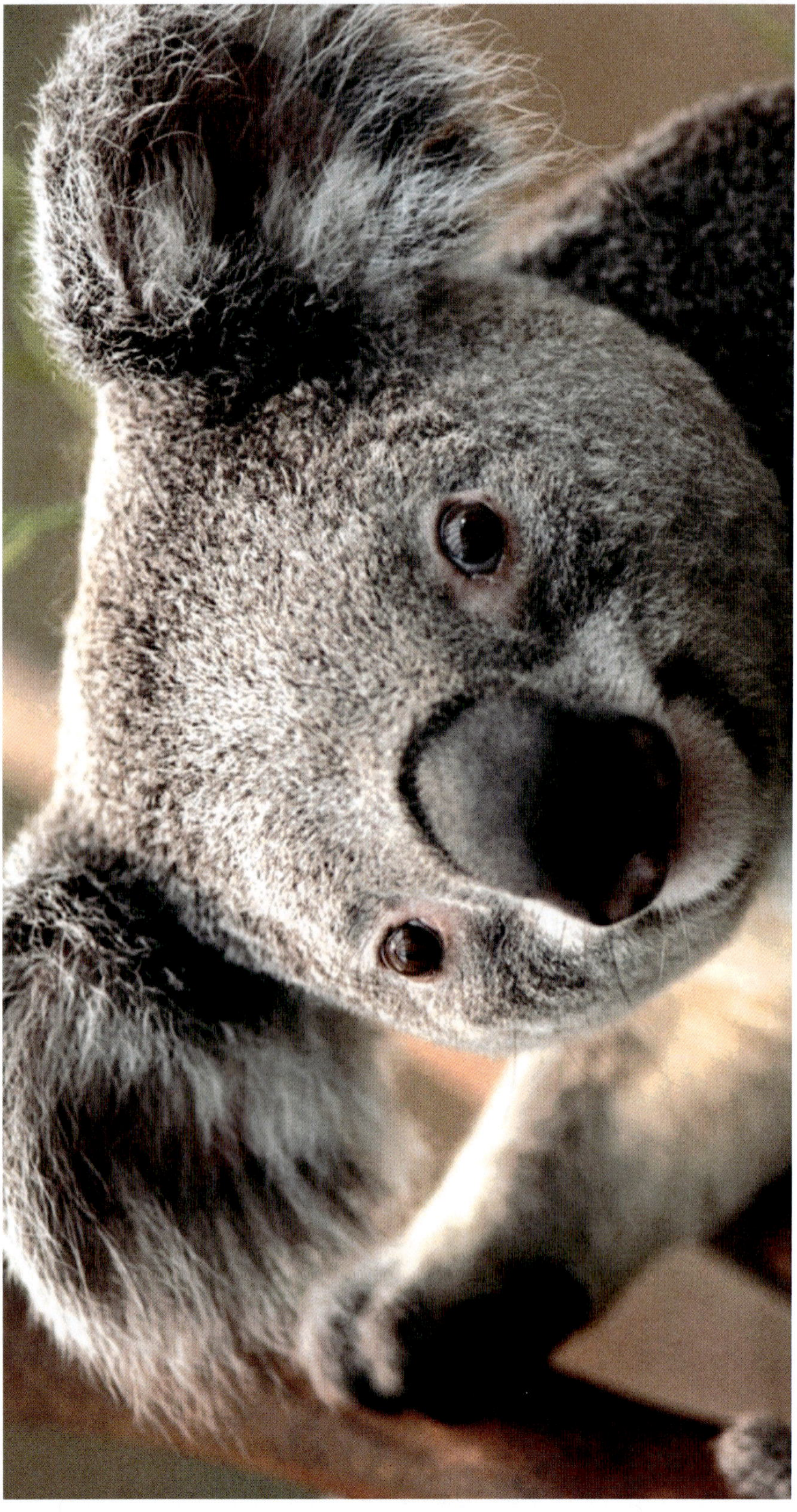

COLOR ME

COLOR ME

COLOR ME

COLOR ME

COLOR ME

COLOR ME

COLOR ME

COLOR ME

COLOR ME

COLOR ME

Please leave me a review here:

LisaStrattin.com/Review-Vol-218

For more Kindle Downloads Visit Lisa Strattin Author Page on Amazon Author Central

amazon.com/author/lisastrattin

To see upcoming titles, visit my website at LisaStrattin.com– most books available on Kindle!

LisaStrattin.com

FREE BOOK

FOR ALL SUBSCRIBERS – SIGN UP NOW

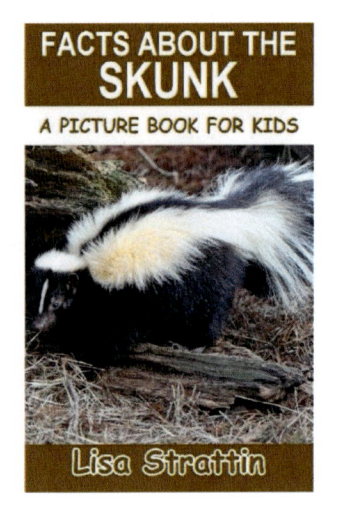

LisaStrattin.com/Subscribe-Here

LisaStrattin.com/Facebook

LisaStrattin.com/Youtube

Made in the USA
Coppell, TX
16 November 2021